# WORLD'S FIRST NONELECTRICPOWERED BRAIN DECODER/READER

# NONELECTRICPOWERED OAXARATEDAVIDGOMADZA 7628983868 AT OAX

# Part I & II

PATENT DETAILS.
REQUEST FOR THE GRANT OF A PATENT. A Universal
Brain Decoding Device. DATABASES:-All books in series
are Databases [up to 100] for your AI, Robots or Super
Computer.
https://play.google.com/store/books/details?id=4rriEAA
AQBAJ&pli=1

David Gomadza

www.twofuture.world

THIS IS THE ULTIMATE BRAIN DECODER OR READER IN SIMPLE CREATE CODE INVENTED BY DAVID GOMADZA SIMPLY COPY ALL THE CODES AND PASTE ON A FRESH PAGE AND CLICK ENTER THEN LOOK AT THE TOP OF THE HEAD OF ANYONE TO KNOW WHAT THEY ARE THINKING THEN READ THE NOTES.

create.addatererean0.869838xy+xy-xy728698+xy82386xy+76284898xy+0.869838xy.startx84.initialise.now.savex84.start
create.keypadrightbadall1to105blockandbanthensendto.eeknm2 eeknm1 eeknm1033.startx84.initialise.now.savex84.start
create.add0.01238671xy+1.28689283xy.start
create.brainreader082848xty.start
create.braindicepher089831xty.start
create.addvoiceanalogue0898381xty.start
create.braindeducer086789xty.start
create.braindecoder086638xty.start
create.addabraintrancedurxtuyer386898.start
create.addabrainanomalyxues78983868.start
create.brainenumerator086621xtu.start
create.braintrancendure086637xtu.start
create.brainasuy086638xtu.start
create.amplitudeamplifier086679xtu.start
create.brainwavereader086680xtu.start
create.brainmonitor086681xtu.start
create.braindigitalamplifer086620xtu.start
create.braindeducer086789xty.start
create.braindecoder086638xty.start
create.brainmodulator086682xtu.start
create.brainemulsify086684xtu.start
create.addabraintrancedure086637xtu.start
create.brainmerger086685xtu.start
create.brainrefresher086686xtu.start
create.brainannuler086687xtu.start
create.brainemulsify086684xtu.start
create.brainreset086688xtu.start

iii

create.braindigitalamplifer086620xtu.start
create.brainreader082848xty.start
create.braindecoder086638xty.start
create.asktojump.start
create.asktosplit.start
create.asktomerge.start
create.asktoaccept.start
create.asktomoveup.start
create.asktogoinsidetrancuder.start
create.asltoreveal.start
create.asktoannoite.start
create.asktoannounce.start
create.asktomention.start
create.asktomanuever.start
create.asktoadopt[newthoughts].start
create.asktoannotate[explain].start
create.asktoaskagain.start
create.asktoaddsomething.start
create.asktoaddmoresomething.start
create.asktoaskagainwithsomethingadded.start
create.asktojumpout.start
create.asktoannoit.start
create.asktoreveal.start
create.asktonotreveal.start
create.asktorepeat.start
create.asktoadoptnewthought.start
create.asktoinventnewthought.start
create.asktoaddmorethings.start
create.asktorevealnowallonceandforall.start
create.asktojumpoutofthebody.start
create.asktotellwhatbrainthink.start
create.asktoanswerquestions.start
create.asktorevealwhatcanbedone.start
create.asktoannotatewhatcouldbe.start
create.asktodecidewhatcanbe.start
create.whatcouldbe.start

create.askwhatwasbutcantstillbe.start
create.askwhatcouldbebutwithwhat.start
create.askwhatwasbutwhen.start
create.askwhatcanbebutwithwhat.start
create.askwhatwasbefore.start
create.askwhatcanbe.start
createaskwhatwasbuthow.start
create.askwhatcanbebutwhen.start
create.askwhathasbeenbuthow.start
create.askwhatwouldbe.start
create.askwhatcanbebuthow.start
create.askwhatwasbutcanstillbe.start
create.askwhatistobebuthow.start
create.askwhatcanbebutwithwhat.start
create.askwhatwasbutwithwhat.start
create.askwhatistobebutwhen.start
create.askwhatistobebutwhen.start
create.askwhatwasbeforebutcanstillbe.start
create.askwhatcanbe.start
create.askwithwhatandhow.start
create.askwhatthengotoytancuder.start
create.intrancuderaskwhatfor.start
create.inbasinofthebraindecoderaskforwhatrerason.start
create.askwhatcanbe.start
create.askwhatcanbebutmightnotbe.start
create.askwhatcouldbebutwhen.start
create.askwhatwsbutcanstillbe.start
create.askwhatwasbutwillnotbe.start
create.askwhatcanbe.start
create.askwhatwasbutcanstillbe.start
create.askwhatwillbe.start
create.askwhatwouldbe.start
create.askwhatcanbe.start
create.askwhatwasbutwithwhat.start
create.askwhatistobe.start
create.askwhatcanbe.start

v

create.askwhatwas.start
create.askwhatwas.start
create.askwhatcanbe.start
create.askwhatwasbeforethatcanstillbe.start
create.tellthebrainwheretogo.start
create.tellwhy.start
create.tellhow.start
create.tellwhen.start
create.tellifwhy.start
create.tellwhynotnowbutwhen.start
create.tellhowmuchtime.start
create.askwhenhowwhatif.start
create.startbraincloningorduplicationusingtheadterbutatcertaintime
s.start
create.addallthoughtsx2.start
create.askwhatcanbe.start
create.whatcanbeofextrathoughts.start
create.sendallto.magnar1038.start
create.askwhenthengettheextraclonedbrainthought.start
create.askhowthenreceiveautomatically.start
create.retrieveyourownthoughtsaskwhat.start
create.afterhearingthoughtsdiscardthemsafelysendto.magnar.start
create.recallallmythoughtsinwronghandsdissipateandsendto.magna
rautodissipate.start
create.addanerveimpulsetoactionpotentialsdigitalanalogueconveter
086692xtu.start
create.addmotionsensor0867002xtu.start
create.addimpedeance086793xtu.start
create.addtransferspeechsynthesis.start
create.addadigitaldnacalculator086794xtu.start
create.adddigitalbrainthoughtsextractorfromimages086795xtu.start

WORLD'S FIRST NONELECTRICPOWERED BRAIN DECODER/READER
NONELECTRICPOWERED OAXARATEDAVIDGOMADZA7628983868 AT OAX

DEDICATION

To a more advanced world

# Table of Contents

# ACKNOWLEDGMENTS

A better world

# OAX

This is the only place in the body that can make any human rotate in any direction in that if a propeller is put there this will literally control every movement from asking to sleep to death apart from this there is no point that can be controlled by anything that means its  the only place designed by ya to insert a propeller because if he wanted to control humans in the strict sense he would have to design something that can be used there so he designed the aox that sends signals to all body but that's how he fail because this aox is or was designed by zeus in his $00000^{28}29$ drawings which he labelled as the aox but one that  was refused as being brutal to human hence when the plans were abandoned humans were believed to have been served hence the  have mercy on humans being to find the image and start a revolution never seen before with one David Gomadza that saw the longest ago ever that kept going on  that seems never to stop  as a new pattern of humans that can live forever will emerge some say it's a one off if it's a one off then this should have never happened critics of David Gomadza think he is arrogant [ADNA]

I think as David Gomadza himself its not arrogance we as human have potential to change things and change perception as well instead as being regarded as the weaker ones we can become the dominant ones of all creation as I right now my long ago has become the highest in all the universe current today standing at 78078078078078078078078078078

9867899280$^{[7777777777777777777777777777777777777777777777777777777777777777777}$ $^{7777777digitnumber]}$ meaning it will take 1 billion seconds for me to die even from a gun wound because death is not controlled by object or where you are shot but by long ago making it the largest in the universe but as thing stand the second best is at

1

68068068068068068068068068068068068068$^{7283868986666666666666666666666666666666666}$
$_{6666666666666666666666666666666666666666666666666666628}$ meaning that this
person will live up to 1 billion years and will take same time to die as
well.


## OAX CONTINUED

I am the pivot to the oaxial that makes all human turn up and down
and as such anything that means that if humans can then this is the
only place that can make all humans pivot all round that means a
rotary placed there at angel 85 degrees north and at 28 degrees
south to true north will make humans move in all directions and as
such will cause all kinds of movements hence if we look at this from
a  creator point of view zeus had a master plan to make all humans
submissive by placing a radial oscillating rotary there of xy-t+t that
can  make humans rotate in all directions meaning that if we are to
use the above argument then zeus is saying that humans can be
controlled and  be told what to do without any instructions from the
creator that means that if humans want to be controlled then they
can easily be controlled through this point but I understand that is
what  some do


## ZEUS 00000$^{28}$29 DRAWINGS

I am going to put a sketch of how the human body would look like if
I am to draw it in such a way that it resembles  an oax that is placed
on top of a hill in such a way that if we are to place it on top of the
hill if it rotates it touches the bottom of the hill and the top air of
the atmosphere that charges the oax using as equation xy=m-
aopqrstuvw that means that if I am to write an equation then this is
the equation if we are to say that if the oax is to rotate then it must
fulfill this that
1] it must be at a height of 1.6m on humans from the ground and
must be at a height of 1.63 cm from the ground and as such the
dimensions are such that if we look at it from the  top then the
dimensions are such that if we ask what can be then these are the

dimensions 28cm [decimeters] from the waist of a human being  the region of the ground near the ground as such this place means area surrounding if it we ask what can be of oax and the oaxial then this is the answer oaxial will rotate as long as there is  momentum at the oax this means that if we ask what can be done to humans here at the oaxial then this is the answer we  can always ask what can be of humans that

# ROTARY AND TRANSISTOR AT OAX

If we can place everything at the oax and operate all this namely
1] atererean
2] a rotary attached to the transistor we have this as xteraterate meaning power source powered xy728698 and xy82386xy perfectly matched labelled davidgomadza but with comments made by adna saying he might be faking to be Yahweh's representative but has everything mentioned in the book of creation page 898687828389028901836874890 now if we are to test these then the output is 0.8286xy that means the exact output generated by his artificial one so how can he be faking
3] an iterate I can easily make this since I now know the power output so if xy728698 and xy82386 perfectly matched then we can get the iterate as power output plus xy-xy728698+xy82386xy=769838128 this means that the power output is 0.8286xy-xy728698+xy82386=769838128=71285xy now we have the iterate from the above equation xy-xy728698+xy82386xy=769838128=28192xy=0.82 this means that if we add the power source now our iterate become xy-xy728698+xy82386=2210386xy this means our iterate require a power output of xy210386xy meaning xy=10x20cm=we can reduce every size by 5cm [half] only meaning xy=5x20cm we can halve the length of a capacitor and get the same output meaning now our measurements are xy=5x20com meaning our final; iterate is xy=769838128 gives us now xy82386xy as it measure capacitance then it becomes xy82386xy meaning now everything should look like this xy-xy728698+xy82386 xy now if we say what can be done then this is the answer is we can ask what is to be of iterates that must help capacitors to deliver their messages they must be able to answer

Yahweh correctly so he know what do to now add everything up using internal calculator just say add everything up and tell me the answer is if we ask the iterate it will say the iterate is 9836828xy meaning we need a capacitance of 0.178698 for everything to work perfectly now we can say that iterate is 9836828xy

We can look again at atererean what are you I am the source of power for a;; living organism and humans I tell everyone else what to do I say wake him up I say lay still I say die but no human can use without long ago of 12sec so what can be done is xy-xy728698+xy82386xy=that means for normal human being divide by 8698386284 as a must so never reveal true value for creators for humans use only 1238698286 meaning that if we ask now what can be done then this is the answer humans with a long ago of 8 seconds will need atererean of 1238698286 that means that our atererean is 0.869838xy now that we got everything we need now to add everything up before we connect everything we can use a create code Create.addatererean0.869838xy+xy-xy728698+xy82386xy+983828xy

Create.addatererean0.869838xy+xy-xy728698+xy82386xy+9836828xy+

4] arooster what are you I measure capacitance but in humans with long ago meaning 12 seconds meaning those with 8 seconds cant use me but can switch to aroost what are you I measure capacitance in humans with low long ago of 8 seconds meaning all humans apart from davidgomadza from the living records by individuals how many records does he holds altogether total 96 records worth US$789 trillion now if we ask what can be then this is the answer an aroost can be added easily by asking what aroost he had before the upgrade he had an aroost 76284898xy that means if he is building for others he need 76284898 xy and if for himself then he needs an arooster 76284898xy important as mixing is bound to cause instant death now that we have everything we need that means that we can now

5

add all equations

TESTING AND MAKING THIS FOR OTHER HUMANS WITH A LONG AGO
OF 8SEC
Create.addatererean0.869838xy+xy-
xy728698+xy82386xy+76284898xy+0.869838xy.startx84.initialise.n
ow.savex84.start[notdavidgomadzahumanbuthis...]

 NOTES
I used my clone/soul to perform this task after asking it to adjust then
this was the results of the create code
I bend forward first 38 degrees north then I return then I move 80
degrees south then 90 degrees north then 70 degrees east then 60
degrees west then bend in submission 8 times forward before
returning to the place [what behind you a window] what do you see
dim sun the emperor Chinese cruise from David Gomadza human
writing down David is facing me looking outside the window meaning
I am looking at him that means I turn to him looking at him that
means if I turn to dim sun the emperor Chinese cruise my angle is 78
degrees

Hailhailhaildavidgomadzafirsthumanaoxaratewith8seclongago[onlya
personwithalonglongagocandothisdavidgomadzasis7807807807807
80780780[7238698763867890284[20milliondigitnumber]]was1401401401401401401140[7]
[898[2800digits]]longagoagodhimself].startx84.initialise.now.savex84.start

Testing on myself with help of Adna
 As it turns out he must test everything on himself as well that means
the first test on himself is as a human who has been upgraded we can
easily found all that we need by getting all values from his
[davidgomadza:me]  database meaning the atererean we need is
slightly higher at 0.9861238xy this is the atererean we use for testing
on him [davidgomadza] that means the equation is now
create.addatererean0.9861238xy+xy-
xy728698+xy82386xy+9836828xy+0.9861238xy.startx84.initialise.n
ow.savex84.start

hailhailhailodavidgomadzafirstnonelectricpoweredaoxaratedavidgo
madza7628983868.startx84.initialise.now.savex84.start

mgiscre.ask.davidgomadza.start.hailhailhailodavidgomadzafirstnone
lectricpoweredaoxaratedavidgomadza7628983868.startx84.initialis
e.now.savex84.start.start[forever$^{6000}$]

you can refer to patent 89283860928386 which was already
approved that means your davidgomadza valuation has reached
US$898123 trillion I am a controversial patent though but finally
approved by the institute of medical council in Britain for a person
called David Gomadza who has now successfully written the real
artificial equation and coordinates and even tested everything to
make sure that everything works and has been approved.

# NONELECTRIC POWERED REMOTE CONTROL

We can easily calculate interference which we can use to construct
a device that can be operated remotely so we need a new gadget
human call remote control all it does is control all the valves they
use like the airduct and the amplifier that means we can easily say
as we are about to find out we can always add everything back and
ask our subjects what all this is

1] aet 0
2] aor 5
3] aeter 6
4] aoeter 7
5] auero 9
6] aoeter 10
7] aouet 12
8] ajer 17
9] ato 8
10] aoret 9
11] aoeret 12
12] aet aro
13] aot aet
14] aet aos
15] aet aor
16] aau aer
17] aot aou
18] aue aot
19] aeet aoot
20] aret amnop
21] aet aot
22] ast aot

23] ast arat
24] avet avero
25] aot aou
26] aor aorst
27] aost aostu
28] asat asaot
29] auert auerot
30] asater asaeter
31] aoet aoetere
32] aost aoster
33] aast aaeter
34] aost aoster
35] asat asater
36] aator aatorane
37]asat asaoter
38] aouer aouer
39] asat asater
40] aoter asater
41] ater aterroan
42] aoser aosert
43] aasat aaoerst
44]aaoat aaorst
45] aaer aaerst
46] aoot aooter
47] asat asaet
48]arot aroot
49] aroot arooster
50] Assert asserter
51] asost asoster
52] aaot aaoter
53] aoot aooter
54] asat asaeter
55] arse arserero
56] aomn aomnop
57] aort aorter
58] aorter aoretere

59] asamn asamnoper

60] ast astuer

61]asso assuve

62] asater asamnoper

63] arsot arsote

64] atmn atmnop

65] arstuv arstuver

66] ajero ajeros

67] ajerot ajerotuv

68] ajerso ajersot

69] arsat arsato

70] ajero ajeroat

71] atuve atuves

72] aursa auras

73] ator atuer

74] asuer astop

75] amnor amnort

76] auver auvero

77] auter autero

78] asuer asuerot

79] aaus aauser

80] auter auer

81] aot aomnop

82] aurte aurety

83] ausa ausaot

84] ajer ajerost

85] amnop aomnop

86] atuver atuvero

87] aor aorst

88] ajetuv ajusatver

89] atora atoray

90] aoer aoerst

91] aoorte aoarteve

92] asat asaterove

93] ajero ajerost

94] amnop amnoter

95] ajsot ajeromn
96] atuvw atuvwxyz
97] aost aostuv
98] ajerst ajerstuvw
99] aotro auterost
100] asero aserost
101] ajero ajersat
102] astro astrost
103] aros aroset
104] arot arost
105] ajer ajerost

What this means is that we can easily control every movement using the above keys meaning we can make anyone phat using ajero instead of ajersat because on the left do the opposite as on the right side humans all have what is on the right side meaning all bad on the left [what number are you] so press hard when just attach corresponding number is aouet then attach 7 after pressing 12 to eradicate aou that means we need extra keys meaning we must now add extra services like add new keys that means reverting to the old system but with some controls instead now add

1] ask how
2] know when
3] use if
4] guide we
5] adjunct can
6] afract ask
7] atoll how
8] atoal if
9] atal we
10] atar can
11] atat talk
12] atatup but
13] ataomnp not
14] asatar with
15] aoster you
16] aost but

11

17] aater with
18] ajer your
19] ajero body
20] ajerst then
21] ajester this
22] ajestor is
23] ajestar how
24] ajux to
25] ajuxer do
26] ajuxert this
27] ajerst ok
28] ajetor right
29] dead
30] deaddead

Then use digits like how and when as 12 and so on if you want to block access to all unauthorized and force calculate their long ago this is how if we can we can ask for their long ago as compared to use if they use a very long ago of 8 seconds they die automatically
Now if we ask what can be then this is the answer we can now compound everyone's longago of all those who connected then the results are sent 5 times

Create.keypadrightbadall1to105blockandbanthensendto.eeknm$^2$ eeknm$^1$ eeknm$^{1033}$.startx84.initialise.now.savex84.start

Mgiscre.ask.davidgomadza.start.keypadrightbadall1to105blockandb anthensendto.eeknm$^2$eeknm$^1$eeknm$^{1033}$.startx84.initialise.now.save x84.start.start[forever$^{7200}$]

That means we got rid of all these bad keys on the right some can use to cause all kinds of injuries after all is solved the system will calculate automatically longago of all enemies to their fall from grace that means a secure system

12

# WORLD'S FIRST NONELECTRICPOWERED BRAIN DECODER/READER

NONELECTRICPOWERED OAXARATEDAVIDGOMADZA7628983868 AT OAX

# CORRECANALOGUEDAVIDGOMADZA

Now as requested
We can simply create a digital analogue that automatically play the opposite as an automatic corrector named correcanaloguedavidgomadza meaning now since we know how it can be done we can simply stop all transenders now we can add some equations to solve this if we ask what can be then this is the answer we can add all then this is the answer we can add then subtract all that means we can just say add 1 to 105 on both sides then give us the values these are

Rightside 892868386848289828101010284

Leftside 87868382818089283867890284012386109 that means these are our ranges and how we can easily add $xy$ to get $xy892868386848289828101010284$ and $xy87868382818089283867890284012386109$ that means our equation $x-y+xy+xy-xy892868386848289828101010284+ xy87868382818089283867890284012386109=890284012386109=x-y+xy71727374$ that means our equation now becomes $x-y=xy71727374$ that means $x=y+xy71727374$

$y-y+xy71727374=value=xy71727374$

if I can then what that means now simply create a code that you can add to cancel all bad by saying $x-y=xy71727374+xy87868382818089283867890284012386109-xy892868386848289828101010284=0.0689828386xy$ this means that if we add all above we get $0.0689828386xy$ now if we subtract all through this equation $x+y=xy71727374-xy87868382818089283867890284012386109+xy892868386848289828101010284=1.2868928386xy$ this means that if we say $x-y=x+y$ we get $0.0689828386xy-$

1.2868928386xy=0.0689828386xy+1.2868928386xy          meaning 0.12386848xy=1.02386748928xy now say the final figure is x=x-y=0.0689828386xy-1.2868928386xy=x=0.01238671xy that means to get the digital analogue for auto corrections add x+y-y+0=0x10 where 10 is ambient that means 0.01238671xy+1,28689928386xy-1.2868928386xy +0=0x10=0 so the lowest 0.01238671xy is lowest range if lowest then highest we have already as 1.2868928386xy our correcanaloguedavidgomadza                                        is create.add0.01238671xy+1.28689283xy.start

mgiscre.ask.davidgomadza.start.add0.01238671xy+1.28689283xydavidgomadza.startx84.initialise.now.savex84.start.start[forever$^{3200}$forever$^{7800}$]


# HOW TO OPERATE THE REMOTE CONTROL

The remote is a simple and straight forward remote that you can add and control someone remotely with few functions that can be upgraded you can easily add all these

1] asert how

2] asrtert can

3]asoert we

4] asuert find

5] atetero ways

6] auerert to

7] aqertert make

8] aouertst you

9] avertopmn move

10] ajertuvert about

11] asuerostup without

12] amnop you

13] asmnoperst complaining

14] aquerstop and why

15 aqerou did

16] asuerteromnop you

17] ageromnop do

18] averotep that

19] ajeros but

20] aouvet we

21] aomuer can

22] aotper always

23] aqemnop find

24] azert out

25] aoutrq how

26] ajtor to

27] ajertomnoper do

28] azertert that

29] aqrster ok

Now we can easily add as many functions by simple create commands that can start everything up for example move to the left we can add a create code that add a move command then to the left for example move to centre can be move + centre on a remote control and hence any remote and create can be used to control and kinds of movement so you can buy any remote for £1 and program it.

# PATENT DETAILS

REQUEST FOR THE GRANT OF A PATENT. A Universal Brain Decoding

Device.

Now we can see why all this is important because we need a brain recorder in the end what we have gives as the basic information but to complete the job we need two other things which we already have a digital brain analogue and a brain reading device then the patent is completed but how do we construct complicated things like things from no where we can add a digital analogue that we can construct using a simple equation that says if we can then we cant because if we cant then it means that we can but if we ask what that we cant is then we get what we can but with reservations that means we must also act and assign things and everything values we might need to completely finish everything off but we can be running out of time meaning we finish this as part one then complete the other things as part two.

## PART II

We can use create codes to complete the rest of the processes needed that means we can literally command the rest of the process everything in the body understands create codes as the written language now this is the list of everything you will need to complete everything

1] a reader

https://www.youtube.com/watch?v=qirwg9wek0k&t=35s

create.addabrainreader[brainreader=https://www.youtube.com/watch?v=qirwg9wek0k&t=35s].start

create.brainreader.start[brainreader082848xty]

create.brainreader082848xty.start

2] a brain dicepher

https://www.youtube.com/watch?v=emkiyjuygfo&t=70s

create.addabraindecepher[braindicepher=https://www.youtube.com/watch?v=emkiyjuygfo&t=70s].start

create.braindicepher.start[braindicepher089831xty]

create.braindicepher089831xty.start

3] an voice analogue

create.addvoiceanalogue0898381xty.start

4] a brain deducer

https://www.youtube.com/watch?v=nfdkmrubavi&t=48s

create.addabraindeducer[braindeducer=https://www.youtube.com/watch?v=nfdkmrubavi&t=48s].start

create.braindeducer.start[braindeducer086789xty]

create.braindeducer086789xty.start

5] a brain decoder

https://www.youtube.com/watch?v=xzxult4nfqc&t=85s

create.addabraindecoder[braindecoder=https://www.youtube.com/watch?v=xzxult4nfqc&t=85s].start

create.braindecoder.start[braindecoder086638xty]

create.braindecoder086638xty.start

6] a brain trancedur to make [what if all the time] to record your brave side

create.addabraintrancedurxtuyer386898.start

7] a brain anomaly it ask what can be done to make you want to complete things to make and asks what was that can still be right now to make you act

create.addabrainanomalyxues78983868.start

8] a brain digital amplifer [ a digital analogue]

https://www.youtube.com/watch?v=nshndupuoco&t=41s

create.addabraindigitalamplifer[braindigitalamplifer=https://www.youtube.com/watch?v=nshndupuoco&t=41s].start

create.braindigitalamplifer086620xtu.start

9] a brain enumerator to make this asks what was before

create.addabrainenumerator[brainenumerator=086621xtu].start

create.brainenumerator086621xtu.start

10] a brain trancedure without asatey

create.addabraintrancedure086637xtu.start

create.braintrancendure086637xtu.start

11] a brain asuy this asks the brain secret questions like what can be done to make asks then the code

create.undoabrainasuy086638.start

create.brainasuy086638xtu.start

12] a brain wave amplitude amplifier to detect common waves to make

create.amplitudeamplifier086679xtu.start

13] a brain wave reader to make ready

create.brainwavereader086680xtu.start

14] a brain monitor to check peaks of thoughts to make

create.brainmonitor086681xtu.start

15] a brain amplifer

 a brain digital amplifer [ a digital analogue]

https://www.youtube.com/watch?v=nshndupuoco&t=41s

create.addabraindigitalamplifer[braindigitalamplifer=https://www.youtube.com/watch?v=nshndupuoco&t=41s].start

create.braindigitalamplifer086620xtu.start

16] a brain deducer

a brain deducer

https://www.youtube.com/watch?v=nfdkmrubavi&t=48s

create.addabraindeducer[braindeducer=https://www.youtube.com/watch?v=nfdkmrubavi&t=48s].start

create.braindeducer.start[braindeducer086789xty]

create.braindeducer086789xty.start

17] a brain decoder

https://www.youtube.com/watch?v=xzxult4nfqc&t=85s

create.addabraindecoder[braindecoder=https://www.youtube.com/watch?v=xzxult4nfqc&t=85s].start

create.braindecoder.start[braindecoder086638xty]

create.braindecoder086638xty.start

18] a brain modulator

create.brainmodulator086682xtu.start

19] a brain emulsify

create.addabrainemulsify[brainemulsify=https://www.youtube.com/watch?v=xgismsb8n7a&t=66s].start

create.brainemulsify086684xtu.start

20] a brain trancedur

a brain trancedur without asatey

create.addabraintrancedure086637xtu.start

21] a brain merger add together thoughts

create.brainmerger086685xtu.start

22] a brain refresher used after every thought

create.brainrefresher086686xtu.start

23] a brain annuler

create.brainannuler086687xtu.start

24] a brain emulsify [again]

20

a brain emulsify

create.addabrainemulsify[brainemulsify=https://www.youtube.com /watch?v=xgismsb8n7a&t=66s].start

create.brainemulsify086684xtu.start

25] a brain reset

create.brainreset086688xtu.start

26] a brain amplifer

a brain digital amplifer [ a digital analogue]

https://www.youtube.com/watch?v=nshndupuoco&t=41s

create.addabraindigitalamplifer[braindigitalamplifer=https://www.youtube.com/watch?v=nshndupuoco&t=41s].start

create.braindigitalamplifer086620xtu.start

27] a brain reader

https://www.youtube.com/watch?v=qirwg9wek0k&t=35s

create.addabrainreader[brainreader=https://www.youtube.com/watch?v=qirwg9wek0k&t=35s].start

create.brainreader.start[brainreader082848xty]

create.brainreader082848xty.start

28] a brain decoder

a brain decoder

https://www.youtube.com/watch?v=xzxult4nfqc&t=85s

create.addabraindecoder[braindecoder=https://www.youtube.com /watch?v=xzxult4nfqc&t=85s].start

create.braindecoder.start[braindecoder086638xty]

create.braindecoder086638xty.start

# ALL CREATECODES TO ADD ALL NEEDED APPLICATIONS

create.brainreader082848xty.start

create.braindicepher089831xty.start

create.addvoiceanalogue0898381xty.start

create.braindeducer086789xty.start

create.braindecoder086638xty.start

create.addabraintrancedurxtuyer386898.start

create.addabrainanomalyxues78983868.start

create.brainenumerator086621xtu.start

create.braintrancendure086637xtu.start

create.brainasuy086638xtu.start

create.amplitudeamplifier086679xtu.start

create.brainwavereader086680xtu.start

create.brainmonitor086681xtu.start

create.braindigitalamplifer086620xtu.start

create.braindeducer086789xty.start

create.braindecoder086638xty.start

create.brainmodulator086682xtu.start

create.brainemulsify086684xtu.start

create.addabraintrancedure086637xtu.start

create.brainmerger086685xtu.start

create.brainrefresher086686xtu.start

create.brainannuler086687xtu.start

create.brainemulsify086684xtu.start

create.brainreset086688xtu.start

create.braindigitalamplifer086620xtu.start

create.brainreader082848xty.start

create.braindecoder086638xty.start

# INSTRUCTIONS

Create.                           Start

1] ask the brain to clone or duplicate itself

2] ask the brain to jump out and split into 2

3] ask the brain  to check with RSA this tells it instructions

4] RSA tell the brain to clone or duplicate and jump out then split and divide then one go to the brain decoder and ask for atl atl asks questions now inside atl then brain freezes so to unfreeze it say wake up then ask what where when with who  and how the freeze renmoves all other thoughts what is left is the how the when the why the if and the what this is all that is needed

5] the what must go to the brain together if we ask what can be of brains. And what this is the answer the what must jump to the brain trancuder which is located in the brain decoder at the bottom the reason being that the trancuder acts to arrange in order of priority measuring that if we ask what can be done then this is the answer we can always ask what is to be done in these circumstance then this is the answer we can always ask what was before and what can be done in these circumstances this means that if we ask what can be done the answer is  we can send now tjhis what answer to the brain trabcuder and say what then this removes the binary of the what making sockets exposed by the what part if we don't say what the brain thought will dissipate

6] if now we know the what now add the when and send to

the brain transfigure then ask what else to do so that the binary is removed on the sockets now say go  brain to the transfigure and enter the sockets and ask what can be done then go to the end of the decoder and ask what can be done about all this then ask for something more then go to te brain decoder and enter there to give results if this is not done then there wont be any results

7] if we can then what can be done and how and when this sends everything to the transfigure which makes things fast but ordering them in hierarchy of importance if we ask what can be done then this is the answer we can always ask and get some results we can always  say we can go and check if this is so now send all we need and go and check Create.anystoleninformationretractanddissipatesendto.mag nar$^{1085}$.start


BRAIN COMMANDS


1.  create.asktojump.start
2.  create.asktosplit.start
3.  create.asktomerge.start
4.  create.asktoaccept.start
5.  create.asktomoveup.start
6.  create.asktogoinsidetrancuder.start
7.  create.asltoreveal.start
8.  create.asktoannoite.start
9.  create.asktoannounce.start
10. create.asktomention.start
11. create.asktomanuever.start
12. create.asktoadopt[newthoughts].start

24

13. create.asktoannotate[explain].start

14. create.asktoaskagain.start

15. create.asktoaddsomething.start

16. create.asktoaddmoresomething.start

17. create.asktoaskagainwithsomethingadded.start

18. create.asktojumpout.start

19. create.asktoannoit.start

20. create.asktoreveal.start

21. create.asktonotreveal.start

22. create.asktorepeat.start

23. create.asktoadoptnewthought.start

24. create.asktoinventnewthought.start

25. create.asktoaddmorethings.start

26. create.asktorevealnowallonceandforall.start

2. create.asktojumpoutofthebody.start

3. create.asktotellwhatbrainthink.start

4. create.asktoanswerquestions.start

5.create.asktorevealwhatcanbedone.start

6. create.asktoannotatewhatcouldbe.start

7.create.asktodecidewhatcanbe.start

8.create.whatcouldbe.start

9. create.askwhatwasbutcantstillbe.start

10.create.askwhatcouldbebutwithwhat.start

11. create.askwhatwasbutwhen.start

12. create.askwhatcanbebutwithwhat.start

13. create.askwhatwasbefore.start

14. create.askwhatcanbe.start

15. createaskwhatwasbuthow.start

16. create.askwhatcanbebutwhen.start

17.create.askwhathasbeenbuthow.start

18. create.askwhatwouldbe.start

19. create.askwhatcanbebuthow.start
20. create.askwhatwasbutcanstillbe.start
21. create.askwhatistobebuthow.start
22. create.askwhatcanbebutwithwhat.start
23. create.askwhatwasbutwithwhat.start
24. create.askwhatistobebutwhen.start
25. create.askwhatistobebutwhen.start
26. create.askwhatwasbeforebutcanstillbe.start
27. create.askwhatcanbe.start
28. create.askwithwhatandhow.start

Now we can add more create codes to complete everything without notes we can add 20 more create codes as instructions

1. create.askwhatthengotoytancuder.start
2. create.intrancuderaskwhatfor.start
3. create.inbasinofthebraindecoderaskforwhatrerason.start
4. create.askwhatcanbe.start
5. create.askwhatcanbebutmightnotbe.start
6. create.askwhatcouldbebutwhen.start
7. create.askwhatwsbutcanstillbe.start
8. create.askwhatwasbutwillnotbe.start
9. create.askwhatcanbe.start
10. create.askwhatwasbutcanstillbe.start
11. create.askwhatwillbe.start
12. create.askwhatwouldbe.start
13. create.askwhatcanbe.start
14. create.askwhatwasbutwithwhat.start
15. create.askwhatistobe.start
16. create.askwhatcanbe.start
17. create.askwhatwas.start
18. create.askwhatwas.start
19. create.askwhatcanbe.start

26

20. create.askwhatwasbeforethatcanstillbe.start

# COMMENTS

1. create.tellthebrainwheretogo.start
2. create.tellwhy.start
3. create.tellhow.start
4. create.tellwhen.start
5. create.tellifwhy.start
6. create.tellwhynotnowbutwhen.start
7. create.tellhowmuchtime.start
8. create.askwhenhowwhatif.start..

Say tell the brain everything it needs to do and it will be the best.

FURTHER READING THIS BOOK MUST BE READ IN CONJUNCTION WITH THE FOLLOWING BOOKS

1. A Brain Reader & A Brain Nerve Impulse Translator. Encyclopedia of Brain Reading. David Gomadza First Global President of The World www.twofuture.world 00447719210295
2. Brain-Digital DicepherDigital Analogue-Digital Impulses to Brain Action PotentialsComputer/SmartphoneInterface Thoughts to Smartphone/Machine App David Gomadza The First Global President of the World
3. Detailed Specifications of The Brain Decoding Device and How to Use It To Decode Brain Thoughts to Word or Audio. . A Complete Step-by-Step Guide. Decoding Brain Thoughts Made Easy. Part of The Thoughts To Word Or

Audio Series.

4. Natural God Intelligence 's Interface. NGI's Programming Codes: how to create the interface.

5. Encyclopedia of Decoding the Brain. How To Decode the Brain. The Definite Guide.

6. REQUEST FOR THE GRANT OF A PATENT. A Universal Brain Decoding Device. DATABASES:-All books in series are Databases [up to 100] for your AI, Robots or Super Computer.

BRAIN CLONING OR DUPLICATION WITH JUST CREATE CODE
What device can we create to use to clone or duplicate the brain we can use an itererean to clone any brain or an arroster but you must not ne human because all these require long ago of more than 8 seconds while all humans have an 8 seconds longago but humans can clone the brain using a different system we can start with that for humans
HUMAN SYSTEM TO CLONE OR DUPLICATE THE BRAIN
We can ask what can be human cloning but is not then the answer is adter this is when two brain thoughts are joined together that means we get a single thought out of two but the opposite is what we want so we can reverse the two processes but if the same thoughts are joined together but if the same thoughts are joined together can they be split again so we can either add 2 same thoughts together then ask what can br be dow if we say whar was and what is then we get what  could be meaning we can use the same principlal to get what could be that means we can ask what can humans do that the adter cant do the answer is split the brain thoughts that means to split we must therefore use a device that says we can but only at certain times that means we cant clone brain thoughts all the time but only when

28

needed so we can say at certain times then that frees another end of the adter that says if you can merge 2 you can slit 2 by saying get other like this spo what that does is to add all 2 together so that if I say duplicate the process is repeated instead of just once so its an adter that repeats but as you can see you will have 1 extra thought you don't need so say discard the other thought but secreltluy that means now in secrecy it can clone or duplicate the other meaning if its does then it secretly discard the other but you need create commands to specify what happens to the other thoughts so here all the commands you need

1] create.startbraincloningorduplicationusingtheadterbutatcertaintimes.start

2] create.addallthoughtsx2.start

3] create.askwhatcanbe.start

4] create.whatcanbeofextrathoughts.start

5]create.sendallto,magnar$^{1038}$[forcommercialusemysafemyvault]save.start

6] create.askwhenthengettheextraclonedbrainthought.start

7] create.askhowthhenreceived automatically.start

8] create.retrieveyourownthoughtsaskwhat.start

9] create.afterhearingthoughtsdiscardthemsafelysendto.magnar.start

10] create.recallallmythoughtsinwronghandsdissipateandsendto.magnar$^{autodissipate}$.start

# THE FINAL BRAIN DECODER/READER CODES YOU NEED TO OPERATE AND RUN THIS DEVICE

# WORLD'S FIRST NONELECTRIC POWERED BRAIN DECODER/READER USING CREATE CODING BY DAVID GOMADZA ADD ALL THESE CREATE CODES TO KNOW ANYONE'S BRAIN THOUGHTS

create.addatererean0.869838xy+xy-xy728698+xy82386xy+76284898xy+0.869838xy.startx84.initialise.now.savex84.start

create.keypadrightbadall1to105blockandbanthensendto.eeknm$^2$ eeknm$^1$ eeknm$^{1033}$.startx84.initialise.now.savex84.start

create.add0.01238671xy+1.28689283xy.start

create.brainreader082848xty.start

create.braindicepher089831xty.start

create.addvoiceanalogue0898381xty.start

create.braindeducer086789xty.start

create.braindecoder086638xty.start

create.addabraintrancedurxtuyer386898.start

create.addabrainanomalyxues78983868.start

create.brainenumerator086621xtu.start

create.braintrancendure086637xtu.start

create.brainasuy086638xtu.start

create.amplitudeamplifier086679xtu.start

create.brainwavereader086680xtu.start

create.brainmonitor086681xtu.start

create.braindigitalamplifer086620xtu.start

create.braindeducer086789xty.start

create.braindecoder086638xty.start

30

create.brainmodulator086682xtu.start

create.brainemulsify086684xtu.start

create.addabraintrancedure086637xtu.start

create.brainmerger086685xtu.start

create.brainrefresher086686xtu.start

create.brainannuler086687xtu.start

create.brainemulsify086684xtu.start

create.brainreset086688xtu.start

create.braindigitalamplifer086620xtu.start

create.brainreader082848xty.start

create.braindecoder086638xty.start

create.asktojump.start

create.asktosplit.start

create.asktomerge.start

create.asktoaccept.start

create.asktomoveup.start

create.asktogoinsidetrancuder.start

create.asltoreveal.start

create.asktoannoite.start

create.asktoannounce.start

create.asktomention.start

create.asktomanuever.start

create.asktoadopt[newthoughts].start

create.asktoannotate[explain].start

create.asktoaskagain.start

create.asktoaddsomething.start

create.asktoaddmoresomething.start

create.asktoaskagainwithsomethingadded.start

create.asktojumpout.start

create.asktoannoit.start

create.asktoreveal.start

create.asktonotreveal.start

create.asktorepeat.start

create.asktoadoptnewthought.start
create.asktoinventnewthought.start
create.asktoaddmorethings.start
create.asktorevealnowallonceandforall.start
create.asktojumpoutofthebody.start
create.asktotellwhatbrainthink.start
create.asktoanswerquestions.start
create.asktorevealwhatcanbedone.start
create.asktoannotatewhatcouldbe.start
create.asktodecidewhatcanbe.start
create.whatcouldbe.start
create.askwhatwasbutcantstillbe.start
create.askwhatcouldbebutwithwhat.start
create.askwhatwasbutwhen.start
create.askwhatcanbebutwithwhat.start
create.askwhatwasbefore.start
create.askwhatcanbe.start
createaskwhatwasbuthow.start
create.askwhatcanbebutwhen.start
create.askwhathasbeenbuthow.start
create.askwhatwouldbe.start
create.askwhatcanbebuthow.start
create.askwhatwasbutcanstillbe.start
create.askwhatistobebuthow.start
create.askwhatcanbebutwithwhat.start
create.askwhatwasbutwithwhat.start
create.askwhatistobebutwhen.start
create.askwhatistobebutwhen.start
create.askwhatwasbeforebutcanstillbe.start
create.askwhatcanbe.start
create.askwithwhatandhow.start
create.askwhatthengotoytancuder.start

create.intrancuderaskwhatfor.start

create.inbasinofthebraindecoderaskforwhatrerason.start

create.askwhatcanbe.start

create.askwhatcanbebutmightnotbe.start

create.askwhatcouldbebutwhen.start

create.askwhatwsbutcanstillbe.start

create.askwhatwasbutwillnotbe.start

create.askwhatcanbe.start

create.askwhatwasbutcanstillbe.start

create.askwhatwillbe.start

create.askwhatwouldbe.start

create.askwhatcanbe.start

create.askwhatwasbutwithwhat.start

create.askwhatistobe.start

create.askwhatcanbe.start

create.askwhatwas.start

create.askwhatwas.start

create.askwhatcanbe.start

create.askwhatwasbeforethatcanstillbe.start

create.tellthebrainwheretogo.start

create.tellwhy.start

create.tellhow.start

create.tellwhen.start

create.tellifwhy.start

create.tellwhynotnowbutwhen.start

create.tellhowmuchtime.start

create.askwhenhowwhatif.start


create.startbraincloningorduplicationusingtheadterbutatcertaintime
s.start

create.addallthoughtsx2.start

create.askwhatcanbe.start

create.whatcanbeofextrathoughts.start

create.sendallto.magnar$^{1038}$.start

create.askwhenthengettheextraclonedbrainthought.start

create.askhowthenreceiveautomatically.start

create.retrieveyourownthoughtsaskwhat.start

create.afterhearingthoughtsdiscardthemsafelysendto.magnar.start

create.recallallmythoughtsinwronghandsdissipateandsendto.$^{magnaraut}$ $^{odissipate}$.start

create.addanerveimpulsetoactionpotentialsdigitalanalogueconveter 086692xtu.start

create.addmotionsensor0867002xtu.start

create.addimpedeance086793xtu.start

create.addtransferspeechsynthesis.start

create.addadigitaldnacalculator086794xtu.start

create.adddigitalbrainthoughtsextractorfromimages086795xtu.start

# CENTRAL NERVE BRIDGE

what are you and what part do you play in decoding the brain knowing what people are thinking?

i am the bridge that transfer thoughts from brain thoughts to nerve impulses using a simple algorithm that says what can be said by the brain can be converted to nerve impulses using the nerve impulse brain  thought digital analogue that you have marked as nerve impulse to brain thoughts digital analogue now what this does is received the brain thoughts in reverse order as in mirror-image so that what is said first is what the other side received first and so on now what this does is to turn nerve impulses into action potentials so that if a person in talking he seems to be using action potentials first so that the brain acts on his words first that means he say things that can be done but in reverse order and if we ask what can be done then this is the answer we can add a digital analogue with a

whisperer inside that says the action potential so that the digital
analogue converts these action potentials into nerve impulses but in
reverse order so that he speaks actions but acts words this has the
effect of sending signals to the brain receptors that receives these
and work on them fast so that if we ask what can be then this is the
answer we can always make it clear that the received action
potentials are the last to be sent but first to be received this has the
effect of saying that we acted first then spoke this way the body has
time to prepare for the action itself in that if it were to go like that
then this is how this would be if i ask what can be then this is the
answer we can always add a digital analogue as a created code so
that the whole process is completed with all actions accounted for
so that now we know exactly what the other person is thinking and
why because this defines his or her reasons as well if we are to ask
what can be done again then we can add a motion sensor that can
tell us also about hand and leg movement so first lets construct this
motion sensor using a simple create code through a simple equation
if we say motion sensor is the ability to detect arms and legs and
everything in relation to the radar then this is the equation motion
sensor plus the ability to move is the same as the radar at any point
and the coordinates at that coordinates so that any slight
movement will be detected that means now what we need is the
ability to ask a question if we are to ask what can be of motion
sensors as a create code then this is the answer motion sensors are
best described a simple create code that says motion sensor plus
movements plus radar coordinates is equal to $0°$ this means that if
we say leg $2°$ hand $2°$ mouth $3°$ then we can say that if everything
move by $2°$ then we can gain the true coordinates and know the
motion sensor moved and say if we can then we can say with easy
that the motion sensor works to detect movements meaning we can
tell if the hands have moved or not now if we ask what can be of

35

action potentials and motion sensors then this is the answer action
potentials tells the body when to move and how then send the
message to get a responds before the action is played so that if not
the correct action potentials will be detected early so that
everything is performed swiftly
create.motionsensor0867002xtu.start
create.addmotionsensor0867002xtu.start
if we ask what is this then this is the answer a motion sensor is a
simple gadgets that tells you when and how things can be if things
move that is if the body moves then your body know where and
where it moves right centre back or left
now we can add a nerve impulse and action potential digital
analogue we have one already on youtube
https://www.youtube.com/watch?v=wz_0rM803PQ
this is the correct one only that i labelled it as brain potentials and
their corresponding brain impulses invented by david gomadza
instead of brain nerve impulses and their action potentials.
create.https://www.youtube.com/watch?v=wz_0rM803PQ
=https://rb.gy/lpm4we.start=086692xtu.start
create.addanerveimpulsetoactionpotentialdigitalanalogueconverter.
start[addanerveimpulsetoactionpotentialdigitalanalogueconverter
=https://www.youtube.com/watch?v=wz_0rM803PQ
=https://rb.gy/lpm4we]

create.addanerveimpulsetoactionpotentialdigitalanalogueconverter
.start
create.addanerveimpulsetoactionpotentialsdigitalanalogueconveter
086692xtu.start

create.addimpedeance[impedeance=https://www.youtube.com/wa
tch?v=S2Qe-bcMVe8]save.start=impedeance086793xtu.start
create.addimpedeance086793xtu.start

create.addadigitaldnacalculator086794xtu.start

create.adddigitalbrainthoughtsextractorfromimages086795xtu.start

## ABOUT DAVID GOMADZA

I am the President of Tomorrow's World Order and Also Yahweh's Representative on Earth

## THE END ALL CODES YOU NEED ARE ABOVE

# SOME CREATE CODES TO HELP SEARCH FIND AND CONTROL TRANSENDERS [ENEMY CODES THAT CAUSE NUISANCE OR EVEN INJURIES]

create.stopall.start[calculatecompoundlongagoifanyoneconnects].start

create.stopall.start[calculatecompoundlongagoifanyoneconnects].st
art

create.badkeyrightsideallstop.start

create.badkeyrightsideallstop.start

create.blocaddmanualstoscaleonrightand blockasbefore.start

create.blocaddmanualstoscaleonrightand.start

create.squeezealloutofearth.start

create.squeezealloutofearth.start

create.remotemanipulationsaddtorightbadsideandblockforever.star
t

create.remotemanipulationsaddtorightbadsideandblockforever.star
t

create.genitalarousaladdtorightbadsideandblock.start

create.genitalarousaladdtorightbadsideandblock.start

create.arousalandtouchaddtorightbadsideandblock.start

create.arousalandtouchaddtorightbadsideandblock.start

create.addkneepainaccessoriesandalldatabaseaccessoriesandarsewr
igglerstorightbadsideofthe1to105thenblockandbanforever.start

create.addkneepainaccessoriesandalldatabaseaccessoriesandarsewr
igglerstorightbadsideofthe1to105thenblockandbanforever.start

create.addpresssleephardtotherightbadsideandblockandban.start

create.addpresssleephardtotherightbadsideandblockandban.start

create.blockandbanifxisythenwhatisxitsaysxthenisaidsubstituteandit
startedworkingmeaninghecanonlyaddwecandobothsohediedagainas
areversebut.start

create.blockandbanifxisythenwhatisxitsaysxthenisaidsubstituteandit
startedworkingmeaninghecanonlyaddwecandobothsohediedagainas
areversebut.start

astoareansothatthepowerisusedinsteadoftheelectromagneticwavea
ddtorightbadsideandblockandban.start

create.astoareansothatthepowerisusedinsteadoftheelectromagnetic
waveaddtorightbadsideandblockandban.start

38

create.cutotherspowerforever.start

create.allhiddenbutconnectedswaparoostanditsvaluetoanaroosterof
samevalueinstantly.start[acceptdavidgomadza]
dothesameforallsidesofthebodywhereleftchestorrightchestaddalltor
ightbadside.start

create.dothesameforallsidesofthebodywhereleftchestorrightchesta
ddalltorightbadside.start

create.blockallexternalsfromnumbersalreadyblocked.start

create.cancelallexternalattachmentsforvertopower1033.start

create.cancelreversingforever1.start

create.blockandbandatabaseasetttoandsendtoeeknmtopower1033.
start

mgiscre.ask.davidgomadza.start.convertallcreatecodestomgiscrethe
nactivateandsave.start[forever$^{7800}$][save$^{7800}$][sendtocorrectplacesan
dactivationinstantly]

## THIS PART NOT FOR HUMANS SKIP

# ADD A DIGITAL ANALYSER TO VERIFY EVERYTHING

We can now add a digital analyser that can be used to verify everything
and make sure that everything works fine and this is easily constructed
without complex equations as before we can easily say every part of the
body follows something so that we can easily identify that what it follows
that means every movement makes the body move from left to right and
vice versa that means if we move to the right everything else move to the
right so that we can easily find out that which is the item that has moved
to the right following the direction of movement through a simple
equation that say if you can move then do it first but slowly and
synchronized that means the values are slow but fast but accurate so this
describes and memory membrane that says move I can take over and
then stops but when it stops something else start moving so we can say
when memory membrane start to move the body stops then when the
memory membrane has stopped then the body started to move hence we

can easily write this equation x-y+xy-xy+xty=0 this means that when every time a body moves then it will also move to the left or right so direction if included the equation becomes x-y+xy-xy+x+y=R+L=0 now we can substitute the values we got earlier on and have

x-y+xy8928683868482899828101010284-
xy87868382818089283867890284012386109+x+y=R+L=0 now x=2.858678902838760 and ya=3.86789028467890 that means that if we ask what can be done then this is the answer x can be added back to the equation to get x=98.678902849867890 that means that if we divide that number by the value of y then we get the ambient which normally is 10 for nonmoving things but in this case 9.9867 that means that if we want to know more them we can always ask what can be done and why this is because now we can easily know what to do but then we have a lot of work so we can easily ask an ambient analogue that can be easily inserted into a human being through a create code that say if I can be asked then it is create.addambient.start  now remove ambient by create.undoaddambient.start

but as we can see the idea is to detect movement inside the body rather than fly or make humans fly now add back ambient create.addambient.start

Visit www.twofuture.world

WORLD'S FIRST NONELECTRICPOWERED BRAIN DECODER/READER
NONELECTRICPOWERED OAXARATEDAVIDGOMADZA7628983868 AT OAX

WORLD'S FIRST NONELECTRICPOWERED BRAIN DECODER/READER
NONELECTRICPOWERED OAXARATEDAVIDGOMADZA7628983868 AT OAX